Contents

STOP
Children working!

"I am a rich man, but I know that there is terrible suffering in our country. Look at our city children! Many live in **slums**. They work every day for long hours. They cannot go out to play. They have no time to eat or sleep and sometimes working makes them ill."

This is wrong! This is the 1800s, and we are modern people. We must change the lives of these poor children! Let me tell you why.

Low pay

" In this day and age, many parents do not earn enough money to support their family. The children must go out to work as well. Many children work from morning until night, but their families are still poor. The children do not get paid very much. "

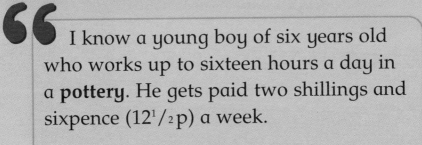

I know a young boy of six years old who works up to sixteen hours a day in a **pottery**. He gets paid two shillings and sixpence ($12^1/_2$p) a week.

Some factory owners say, 'Everyone knows that workers must be kept poor or they will never work hard.' They are wrong to say such things. If people work hard, they should be paid enough to live on.

Long hours

Factory owners like children to work for them. Why? Because children are cheap workers. They work long hours for little money. The longer children work, the richer the factory owner becomes. Now who is going to stop this? The children cannot, because no one will listen to them.

One young girl in Bradford gets up at two o'clock in the morning. She gets dressed and walks to work at the **mill**. She is allowed a cup of tea. Then she must work for fifteen hours! She gets home very late at night and falls asleep over her small supper. She needs more rest, and more time to eat.

PROFILE

HANNAH BROWN **BORN IN BRADFORD IN 1809.**

Question: How early did you begin to work in mills?
Answer: At nine years old.
Question: What hours did you work?
Answer: I began at six o'clock, and worked till nine at night.
Question: What time was allowed for your meals?
Answer: None at all.

Extract from interview for House of Commons in 1832.

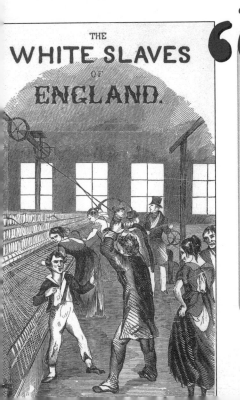

Do you think it is right that a small child sleeps only four hours a night? I don't think so. And working children are punished if they try to rest. They are fined for whistling, or beaten with a strap. I have heard that young boys in one of the mills have to be silent for eleven hours each day!

Children get ill

> Children work in mines, in mills, in factories, in the potteries, and up chimneys. They get tired and weak. I have seen shocking things. Eleven thousand young children get ill from working in the potteries!

> A six-year-old chimney sweep gets ill from breathing in soot. The soot rubs into his knees and elbows which are grazed from climbing the chimneys. Young **matchgirls** get an illness which makes their bones crumble. Many children cough and cough after working long hours in dark and dusty mills.

PROFILE

**ELIZABETH BENTLEY
BORN IN LEEDS
IN 1809.**

Question: What is working in the mill like?
Answer: Dusty. You cannot see each other for dust.
Question: Did working in the card-room affect your health?
Answer: Yes; it was so dusty, the dust got up my lungs, and the work was so hard. I got so bad in health, that when I pulled the baskets down, I pulled my bones out of their places.

Extract from interview for House of Commons in 1832.

> " I hear mill owners say, 'We are helping children by giving them work.' But they are not helping the children who get ill from the work they do. "

DID YOU KNOW?

 Dust and fibres from cotton caused many different lung diseases and made breathing difficult for children in the mills.

Danger!

"I have heard horrible stories. In a dark tunnel of a deep mine, a little boy of six sits alone for twelve hours a day, opening a trap door to let wagons pass by. If he falls asleep at work, he could be killed because the tunnels sometimes flood with water, or the tunnel roof may collapse on top of him."

"The mills are dangerous too. Small children have to crawl underneath the **looms** to clear fluff from the floor. The loom is still working. Many girls have been caught in these machines and killed.

And little boys are suffocated or burned to death in chimneys."

"There should be more laws against this cruelty. The Earl of Shaftesbury agrees. He fights in Parliament to help protect working children. I hope he wins for the sake of the children!"

No time to play

> Children from rich families have time to play games, to sing, to run and draw. But when do poor children play? They have to work, some of them for fourteen hours a day. After that they are too tired for games.

'We want time for more rest, a little play, and to learn to read and write,' say the children.

Some children from Manchester wrote to the government asking for help in 1836.

'We have factories to run,' say the mill owners. 'If working children don't work hard, then they will starve. Do they want to have fun, or do they want to eat?'
I believe that children should have fun *and* enough food to eat.

No time for school

"Rich children are taught by teachers at home or at a school. Many poor children cannot even write their names. They cannot stop working and go to school. If they stop working, how can they eat? They will have no money to pay for food. But if they do not go to school, how will they learn to read and write?"

Some factory owners think that poor children should never learn to read or write. They say, 'If children are educated they will say it is our fault that they are poor and unhappy. It is better that they never go to school.'

I say it isn't fair to stop them learning to read and write.

No time for family life

> **When can working children see their families? Never!**
>
> Factory machines can work all day without getting tired. Children are small and fast. They must earn as much as they can for their families, so they work long hours. What time is there left for children to see their parents and their brothers and sisters?

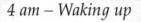

4 am – Waking up

5 am – Arrive at the Wool Mill

> The father is often a **labourer** who works twelve hours or more each day. Maybe the mother works on the machines at a factory all day. There is no time for them to care for their children.

> Factory owners say, 'Children should be happy to have a job at all. There are plenty more who will work long hours if these children want to go off and see their families!' But shouldn't every child have the right to spend time with his or her family?

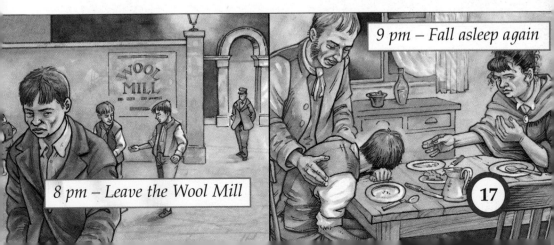

8 pm – Leave the Wool Mill

9 pm – Fall asleep again

Short working lives

No of workers

1169

736

612

11-16   17-21   22-26

Age of workers

" Children start work as soon as their parents will let them, but their working lives may be very short. Children are paid less than half what a man is paid, so they are cheap workers. But when they grow up, what happens? When they reach seventeen or eighteen years old, many **employers** will not pay them proper wages, so they lose their jobs. It is the same everywhere. "

> I say it is wrong to throw young people out of work when they are seventeen or eighteen. They still need a job and a wage. Better still, give men and women proper wages for their work, so that they can feed their families and don't have to send their children out to work at all!

The employers want the cheapest workers available.

Workhouse children need help!

> " If mine owners or factory owners need more child workers, what do they do? They take children from the **workhouses** to work for them. "

> But workhouses are cruel places. Families are often split up, so men, women and children do not live together. Many children die in workhouses. It is not fair to treat the poorest children this way and then make them work in terrible conditions as well.

When things go wrong ...

"What happens to the working children:

- if they get ill and can't work?

- if they lose their jobs?

- if the price of bread goes up and wages are cut so that they can't afford to buy any?"

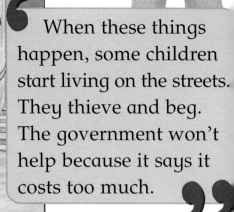

"When these things happen, some children start living on the streets. They thieve and beg. The government won't help because it says it costs too much."

The government says, 'We have already built workhouses to help the poor. Poor families can work in the workhouse, get food, a bed to sleep in, and education for the children. What else can we do?'

But the children say workhouses are like prisons. They are made to work like slaves, given bad food, and their families are split up, mothers and fathers living apart from their children. This is no way for children to live.

Workhouses were overcrowded.

"Now that you have heard my speech, I'm sure you agree with me that working children need help.

- They work long hours but are paid less than half an adult's wages.

- The work they do is often dangerous, or makes them ill.

- They work so many hours that there is no time for playing as all children should do, and no time for family life.

- At the age of seventeen, these young people can lose their jobs because their employers will not pay them the adult wages they deserve."

> " Think of these poor children and join me in my **campaign** to speak out against the people who hurt them. "

What was being done?

Not all factory owners were bad. A few people in the country had been persuaded by these arguments and were already helping these working children.

Sir Titus Salt was such a man. He built a large and airy mill in Yorkshire so that his workers were happy at work.

He has built large cottages for the workers to live in. He also built a school and a church for them.

Companies like Cadbury and Rowntree treated their workers better, and they are still around today!

Mr Robert Owen was another good man. He built a village and a school for his mill workers in New Lanark in Scotland.

Mr Cadbury and Mr Rowntree, who made chocolate and sweets, also looked after their workers well.

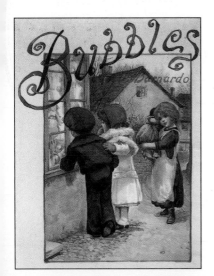

Other people were also trying to help poor children.

Dr Thomas Barnardo built homes for **orphans**.

Barnardo's homes still take in homeless children today.

New laws?

The government took notice of the working children too. The Earl of Shaftesbury was one of the men working to change laws to save children from harm in factories, mines and chimneys, and to give them a proper education.

Shaftesbury set up the Children's Employment Commission. In 1842 the commission printed a report describing the bad conditions children had to suffer in the coal mines. The report shocked the country. Most people did not realise that children were being used as miners. This report helped Shaftesbury put together an important new law that stopped children from working in mines in Britain.

Thanks to people like The Earl of Shaftesbury more and more laws were passed to protect working children.

Laws passed to help working children

1819 The **Factory Act** stopped children under the age of nine from working in the cotton mills.

1833 The **Factory Act** said that:
- no child under the age of nine should work in textile mills
- children aged between nine and thirteen should work only nine hours each day
- children up to the age of thirteen should receive half-time schooling each week
- factory inspectors should check that this law was being obeyed

1842 The **Mines Act** said that women and young girls and boys under the age of ten should not work underground.

1844 The **Factory Act** said that:

- children aged between nine and thirteen should work only six and a half hours a day
- young people (aged between thirteen and eighteen), and women should work only twelve hours a day
- dangerous machines should be guarded

1847 The **Ten Hours Act** said that young people under the age of eighteen and women who work in factories should work only ten hours a day.

1870 Forster's **Education Act** introduced schools managed by school **boards**. The school boards could make any child up to the age of thirteen go to school.

1880 Mundella's **Education Act** said that all children aged between five and ten must go to school.

Glossary

board a specially chosen group of people who meet to talk about how to run things properly

campaign an organised way of making your views known to people or governments

employers people who pay other people to work for them

labourer a person who does heavy unskilled work using muscle power

loom a machine that weaves thread into cloth.

matchgirls young girls who made matches from slips of wood and dangerous chemicals

mill a big factory building full of machines that make cloth

orphans children whose parents have died

pottery a workshop or factory where clay is shaped and fired into finished pots or plates, etc

slums dirty overcrowded parts of cities, where houses are unfit to live in

workhouse a Victorian public building where people with no money or jobs could stay in return for work

Index